Contents

Words shown in the text in bold, **like this**, are explained in the Glossary.

Eating at restaurants

All around the world, people like to eat at restaurants. Different kinds of restaurants serve different kinds of food.

Some restaurants serve smart meals that cost a lot of money.

This is Ray Kroc in front of one of his early restaurants.

Fast food restaurants serve meals quickly. The food costs less than it does at a smart restaurant. Ray Kroc helped to make fast food popular when he started the McDonald's restaurant **chain**.

The early years

Here is Ray
with his mother
and sister.

Ray Kroc was born in Oak Park, Illinois,
USA, in 1902. As a boy, he loved **baseball**
and playing the piano. Ray's mother was
a piano teacher and she gave him lessons.

Ray liked to work. He sold lemonade to make money. When he got older, he worked in a grocer's shop and a chemist. He even started a music shop with his friends.

Even as a little boy, Ray liked selling things to people.

Growing up

When Ray was fifteen, the USA was fighting in **World War 1**. Ray lied about his age so that he could train to be an **ambulance** driver. He wanted to help people who had been hurt.

By the time Ray finished his training, the war was over.

Ray went back to school, but he left before he finished. Then he got a job selling ribbons. He also earned extra money by playing the piano at night.

Ray travelled from place to place to sell ribbons.

9

Becoming a salesman

In 1922, Ray started a new job selling paper cups to restaurants. Ray worked hard and became one of the company's best **salesmen**.

Restaurants bought paper cups for serving drinks.

The Multimixer made it easier to make milkshakes.

One of Ray's **customers** invented a machine called the Multimixer. It could make five milkshakes at once! In 1939, Ray started his own business selling the machine.

The McDonald brothers

Ray travelled around the USA selling Multimixers. Many of his **customers** in Southern California talked about a restaurant called McDonald's.

Mac and Dick McDonald used eight Multimixers in their restaurant!

Why did the McDonald brothers need so many Multimixers? Ray parked outside their restaurant and watched. Many people came to buy hamburgers and milkshakes.

The original McDonald's only had a few things on the menu.

A big idea

McDonald's Speedee Service
MENU

HAMBURGERS	15¢
CHEESEBURGERS	19¢
MALT SHAKES	20¢
FRENCH FRIES	10¢
ORANGE	10¢
ROOT BEER	10¢
COFFEE	10¢
COKE	10¢
	10¢

A small menu helped McDonald's to make food quickly and cheaply.

Ray thought that Mac and Dick should start a **chain** of restaurants. But the brothers did not want a lot of restaurants. They agreed to let Ray start the chain.

14

Mac and Dick agreed to show Ray how they ran their restaurant. Ray would then open more McDonald's restaurants and give the brothers some of the money.

Every McDonald's restaurant was to have golden **arches**.

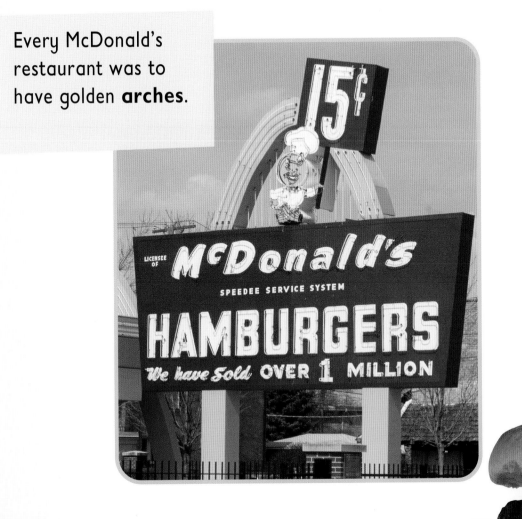

A new company

In 1954, Ray opened his first McDonald's restaurant. He wanted to have many more restaurants, but he could not do this alone. He started a company that sold **franchises** to other people.

Ray's first restaurant was in Des Plaines, Illinois.

Anyone who bought a franchise could open a McDonald's. Ray's company would help them set up their restaurants. By 1957, there were 38 McDonald's in the USA.

Ray (on the right) planned many new restaurants.

McDonald's grows

Ray worked very hard for his company. He expected his staff to work hard, too. Ray thought that the bosses should know how to do every job their workers did.

Ray helped to keep his restaurants clean. In this photo, he is washing a pavement.

Hamburger University teaches groups of new students about the restaurant business.

Ray wanted all McDonald's restaurant owners to be successful. He started a school called Hamburger University. People went there to learn how to run a **fast food** restaurant.

New ideas

Ray looked for ideas to make his company grow. Saving time by using hamburger buns that were already sliced was one idea. Having a clown called Ronald McDonald was another.

Ray added new foods to the menu. But McDonald's was best known for its hamburgers.

Another new idea was to have McDonald's restaurants outside the USA. Since 1967, a new McDonald's restaurant has opened in a new country almost every year.

Ray was there when the first McDonald's was opened in Munich, Germany.

Helping others

Ray (in the middle) gave money to people who wanted to help others.

Ray raised money to help fight **diseases.** On his birthday in 1972, he gave millions of dollars to hospitals, churches, libraries, **museums**, and other places.

Ray also helped others by giving them a chance to work for his company. In 1972, he got a special award for the opportunities he gave to young people.

Ray is on the left, being given the Horatio Alger Award.

Reaching out

Ray wanted McDonald's workers to help people, too. In 1974, McDonald's owners in Philadelphia, USA, helped to start a house for the families of sick children. It was called the Ronald McDonald House.

The families of sick children could stay at the Ronald McDonald House for free.

RONALD MCDONALD HOUSE

DEDICATED

OCTOBER 15, 1974

The Ronald McDonald House in Indianapolis, USA, opened in 1982.

Ray's company showed people how to set up new Ronald McDonald Houses in their towns. For Ray's 75th birthday, his friends started a **fund**. It helped to build Ronald McDonald Houses all over the USA.

A baseball dream

In 1974, Ray heard that the San Diego Padres **baseball** team was for sale. People were afraid the team would be sold to another city. Ray decided to buy it.

Ray enjoyed going to the Padres baseball games.

In 1984, the Padres played in the biggest baseball competition – the World Series. But Ray did not get to see them play. Sadly, he had died earlier that year.

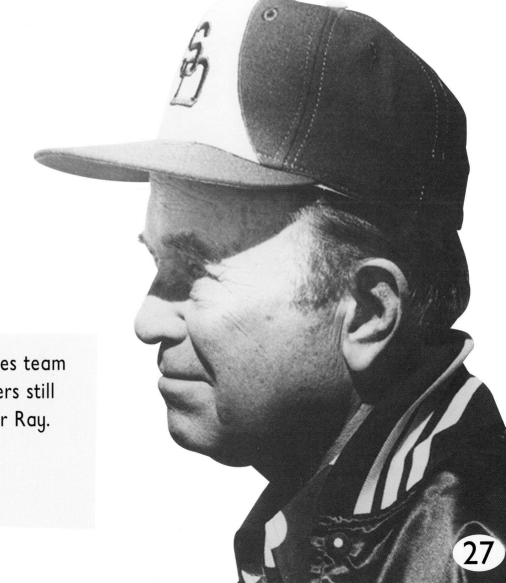

The Padres team and players still remember Ray.

27

More about Ray

McDonald's is popular all over the world.
This restaurant is in Indonesia.

Ray Kroc's dream of running a **chain** of restaurants came true. By 2003, there were 30,000 McDonald's restaurants in 121 countries around the world.

Ray's first restaurant in Des Plaines is now a **museum**. People can visit it to learn about Ray and the company he started.

Museum displays show what the restaurants looked like when they first opened.

Fact File

- When Ray Kroc started McDonald's, he had trouble making French fries. He worked for three months to get them right.

- Ray Kroc's goal was to sell a hamburger, milkshake, and fries to a **customer** in less than one minute.

- The words "Quality, Service, and Cleanliness" were used in McDonald's advertising for the first time in 1957.

- Ray Kroc became a member of the Advertising Hall of Fame in 1988. He was made a member because of his hard work and success, and the help he gave to other people.

Timeline

1902	Ray Kroc is born in Oak Park, Illinois, USA
1922	Ray begins to sell paper cups
1938	Ray begins to sell Multimixers
1955	Ray opens his first McDonald's restaurant in Des Plaines, Illinois, USA
1961	Hamburger University opens
1967	First McDonald's restaurants open outside the USA
1972	Ray gives away US $7.5 million (£4.1 million) to help others
1974	Ray buys the San Diego Padres **baseball** team; first Ronald McDonald House opens in Philadelphia, USA; first McDonald's opens in the UK
1984	Ray Kroc dies

Glossary

ambulance vehicle used to carry people to hospital

arch something with a curved shape

baseball American ball game played between two teams, using a bat and a ball

chain group of businesses with the same name and product

customer someone who buys a product or service

disease sickness

fast food food that is served quickly and does not cost a lot

franchise right to sell a company's products and use its name

fund sum of money used for a special purpose

museum place where pieces of art or important parts of history are kept

salesmen people who sell things to other people

World War I war fought from 1914 to 1918 that involved European countries and the USA

Find out more

Look After Yourself: Healthy Food, Angela Royston (Heinemann Library, 2003)

The Life of H.J. Heinz, M.C. Hall (Heinemann Library, 2003)

> Always remember that eating too much 'fast food' is bad for your health.

Index